THE KINGDOM OF ORDINARY TIME

THE KINGDOM OF

ORDINARY TIME

★

Marie Howe

W. W. NORTON & COMPANY
NEW YORK • LONDON

For information about permission to reproduce selections from this book,
write to Permissions, W. W. Norton & Company, Inc.,
500 Fifth Avenue, New York, NY 10110

For information about special discounts for bulk purchases,
please contact W. W. Norton Special Sales at specialsales@wwnorton.com or 800-233-4830

Manufacturing by The Courier Companies, Inc.
Book design by Chris Welch Design
Production manager: Andrew Marasia

Library of Congress Cataloging-in-Publication Data

Howe, Marie, 1950–
The kingdom of ordinary time / Marie Howe.— 1st ed.
p. cm.
ISBN 978-0-393-04199-6 (hardcover)
I. Title.
PS3558.O8925K56 2008
811'.54—dc22

2007040489

ISBN 978-0-393-33734-1 pbk.

W. W. Norton & Company, Inc.
500 Fifth Avenue, New York, N.Y. 10110
www.wwnorton.com

W. W. Norton & Company Ltd.
15 Carlisle Street, London W1D 3BS

10 11 12 13 14 15

Acknowledgments

Thank you to the magazines and anthologies where some of these poems first appeared:

"The Star Market" and "Marriage" were first published in *The New Yorker*.

"The Spell" was first published in *MS*. Magazine.

"Annunciation" was first published in *Dancing with Joy*, edited by Roger Housden.

"Courage" and "Non-violence 2" are included in the anthology *Not for Mothers Only: Contemporary Poems in Child-Getting and Child-Rearing*, edited by Catherine Wagner and Rebecca Wolff.

"That Massacre" first appeared in *A Memory, a Monologue, a Rant and a Prayer*, edited by Eve Ensler and Mollie Doyle.

"Poems from the Life of Mary" were first published in a chapbook produced by the Center for Book Arts, New York City.

This book would not have come into being without the daily friendship, encouragement, and support of Jason Shinder.   Thank you for every minute.

Thank you to dear friends and close readers Michael Cunningham, Mark Doty, Brenda Hillman, Tony Hoagland, Paul Lisicky, Donna Masini, Richard McCann, and Tom Sleigh for their specific comments on the poems.

Thank you to Jill Bialosky for her careful gracious attention to this collection.

Thank you to Beth Howe Madden, Dorothy Howe Kelley, and Annika Shore for time.

Thank you to Alex Ross and Grace Yi-Nan Howe for the cover painting.

For Grace Yi-Nan Howe

In memory of Jane Crowley Howe

★

Contents

Prologue

The rules, once again, applied
One loaf = one loaf. One fish = one fish.
The so-called Kings were dead.

And the woman who had been healed grew tired of telling her story,
and sometimes asked her daughter to tell it.

People generally worshipped where their parents had worshipped—
the men who'd hijacked the airplane prayed where the dead pilots had been sitting,
and the passengers prayed from their seats
—so many songs went up and out into the thinning air . . .

People, listening and watching, nodded and wept, and, leaving the theater,
one turned to the other and said, What do you want to do now?
And the other one said, I don't know. What do you want to do?

It was the Coming of Ordinary Time. First Sunday, second Sunday.
And then (for who knows how long) it was here.

The World

I couldn't tell one song from another,
  which bird said what or to whom or for what reason.

The oak tree seemed to be writing something using very few words.
  I couldn't decide which door to open—they looked the same, or what

would happen when I did reach out and turn a knob. I thought I was safe,
  standing there
but my death remembered its date:

only so many summer nights still stood before me, full moon, waning moon,
  October mornings: what to make of them? which door?

I couldn't tell which stars were which or how far away any one of them was,
  or which were still burning or not—their light moving through space like a
  long

late train—and I've lived on this earth so long—50 winters, 50 springs and
  summers,
and all this time stars in the sky—in daylight

when I couldn't see them, and at night when, most nights, I didn't look.

The Star Market

The people Jesus loved were shopping at The Star Market yesterday.
An old lead-colored man standing next to me at the checkout
breathed so heavily I had to step back a few steps.

Even after his bags were packed he still stood, breathing hard and
hawking into his hand. The feeble, the lame, I could hardly look at them:
shuffling through the aisles, they smelled of decay, as if The Star Market

had declared a day off for the able-bodied, and I had wandered in
with the rest of them: sour milk, bad meat:
looking for cereal and spring water.

Jesus must have been a saint, I said to myself, looking for my lost car
in the parking lot later, stumbling among the people who would have
been lowered into rooms by ropes, who would have crept

out of caves or crawled from the corners of public baths on their hands
and knees begging for mercy.

If I touch only the hem of his garment, one woman thought, I will be healed.
Could I bear the look on his face when he wheels around?

Reading Ovid

The thing about those Greeks and Romans is that
   at least mythologically,

they could get mad. If the man broke your heart, if he
   fucked your sister speechless

then real true hell broke loose:
   "You know that stew you just ate for dinner, honey?—

It was your son."
   That's Ovid for you.

A guy who knows how to tell a story about people who
   really don't believe in the Golden Rule.

Sometimes, I fantasize saying to the man I married, "You know
   that hamburger you just

gobbled down with relish and mustard? It was
   your truck."

If only to watch understanding take his face
   like the swan-god took the girl.

But rage makes for more rage—nothing to do then but run.
  And because rage is a story that has

no ending, we'd both have to transform into birds or fish:
  constellations forever fixed

in the starry heavens, forever separated,
  forever attached.

Remember the story of Athens and Sparta?
  That boy held the fox under his cloak

and didn't flinch. A cab driver told me the part
  I couldn't remember this morning—

in Sparta, he said, it was permissible to steal
  but not to get caught.

The fox bit and scratched; the kid didn't talk,
  and he was a hero.

Do unto others as you would have them do unto you,
  Jesus said. He said, The kingdom of heaven

is within you.

And the spiked wheel ploughed through the living centuries

minute by minute, soul by soul. Ploughs still. That's the good news
and the bad news, isn't it?

Would You Rather

My sister told me that when she was giving birth every time a contraction
    passed
she was surprised she was still conscious, proud that she hadn't passed out.

The guy on The Nature Channel said that the anaconda tried to eat the large
    gazelle,
but when his mouth got to the wide horns, he stopped.

High over the city now, one silver airplane flying towards Europe, towards the
    past.
Some of the people on the plane must be reading the newspaper, holding the
    pages

out in front or reading the paper folded as if the plane were a subway.
And the woman shot running with her two children towards the forest, shot
    with one

child in her arms is a story someone on the plane is reading. The other child,
    running
behind her, shot too—her body found on the path 2 or 3 feet behind her
    mother's.

And the baby apparently shot where he fell.
The anaconda will eat the gazelle until his mouth knocks against the horns his
    mouth

isn't wide enough to admit—then its jaws unhinge and widen.
The man said the anaconda will admit the horns even if they rip its body open

from the inside. Would you rather be the woman? Or one of the soldiers?
The baby? Or the soldier who shot and bayoneted the baby when he got there?

After the Movie

My friend Michael and I are walking home arguing about the movie.
He says that he believes a person can love someone
and still be able to murder that person.

I say, No, that's not love. That's attachment.
Michael says, No, that's love. You can love someone, then come to a day

when you're forced to think "it's him or me"
think "me" and kill him.

I say, Then it's not love anymore.
Michael says, It was love up to then though.

I say, Maybe we mean different things by the same word.
Michael says, Humans are complicated: love can exist even in the murderous
 heart.

I say that what he might mean by love is desire.
Love is not a feeling, I say. And Michael says, Then what is it?

We're walking along West 16th Street—a clear unclouded night—and I hear
 my voice
repeating what I used to say to my husband: Love is action, I used to say to
 him.

Simone Weil says that when you really love you are able to look at someone
   you want to eat and not eat them.

Janis Joplin says, take another little piece of my heart now baby.

Meister Eckhart says that as long as we love any image we are doomed to live
   in purgatory.

Michael and I stand on the corner of 6th Avenue saying goodnight.
I can't drink enough of the tangerine spritzer I've just bought—

again and again I bring the cold can to my mouth and suck the stuff from
the hole the flip top made.

What are you doing tomorrow? Michael says.
But what I think he's saying is "You are too strict. You are a nun."

Then I think, Do I love Michael enough to allow him to think these things of
   me even if he's not thinking them?

Above Manhattan, the moon wanes, and the sky turns clearer and colder.
Although the days, after the solstice, have started to lengthen,

we both know the winter has only begun.

Limbo

Each of them can't decide if there is a God
or if there is a self.

Do I have an I? one says
to another who seems distracted, looking out what might have been a window.

What is the difference between a self and a soul?
Is it true that one god is in relationship to each of us?
Or is the each of us an illusion, and we are the god we are looking for?
        That's what the distracted one is thinking and what
she wants to know,

and she wishes that other person would stop bothering her,
and she wishes she had more time to think about these things,
although she has all the time in the world.

Easter

Two of the fingers on his right hand
had been broken

so when he poured back into that hand it surprised
him—it hurt him at first.

And the whole body was too small. Imagine
the sky trying to fit into a tunnel carved into a hill.

He came into it two ways:
From the outside, as we step into a pair of pants.

And from the center—suddenly all at once.
Then he felt himself awake in the dark alone.

Marriage

My husband likes to watch the cooking shows, the building shows,
the Discovery Channel, and the surgery channel.
Last night he told us about a man who came into the emergency room

with a bayonet stuck entirely through his skull and brain.
Did they get it out? We all asked.
They did. And the man was ok because the blade went exactly between

the two halves without severing them.
And who had shoved this bayonet into the man's head? His wife.
A strong woman, someone said. And everyone else agreed.

The Tree Fort

It stood beyond our boundaries
but we didn't know that until the lot next door was sold

—the wooded field had a line drawn through it that put the tree
and what our father had built for us—on the side of strangers.

But no matter how we pleaded they tore the painted planks and platform up
and the ladder and the tree came down.

And when we thrashed through the high weeds indignant, beholden to no one
we came upon the girl standing in the clearing. This is our land, she said.

and she had a gun,—a toy gun, an air rifle, the kind we had at home—
and shoved the muzzle down in the dirt and raised it and cocked it.

And so we learned a new art, standing there,
although we threatened and posed—progress stood between us. The tree fort

was gone. The tractors and the builders took the field, their house rose up
split-level, glass and modern. Her father muttered in Italian.

Her mother, small and coifed looked nothing like our mother. And Gloria
became our neighbor, if not our friend.

Prayer

Every day I want to speak with you. And every day something more important
calls for my attention—the drugstore, the beauty products, the luggage

I need to buy for the trip.
Even now I can hardly sit here

among the falling piles of paper and clothing, the garbage trucks outside
already screeching and banging.

The mystics say you are as close as my own breath.
Why do I flee from you?

My days and nights pour through me like complaints
and become a story I forgot to tell.

Help me. Even as I write these words I am planning
to rise from the chair as soon as I finish this sentence.

Courage

I'm helping my little girl slide down the pole next to the slide-and-bridge
    construction
when a little boy walks up and says, Why are you helping that young person
do something that's too dangerous for her?

Why do you say it's too dangerous? I say
And he says, She's too young.
And I say, How old are you? And he says, four and a half.
And I say, Well, she's three and a half

When he comes back a little later he says, I'll show you how it's done, and
    climbs up the ladder and slides down the pole.
Then he says, She's too young. What happens is that when you get older you
    get braver.
Then he pauses and looks at me, Are you brave?

Brave? I say, looking at him.
Are you afraid of Parasite 2? he says.
And I say, What's Parasite 2?
And he walks away slowly, shaking his head.

Why the Novel Is Necessary but Sometimes Hard to Read

It happens in time. *Years passed until the old woman,*
one snowy morning, realized she had never loved her daughter . . .

Or, *Five years later she answered the door, and her suitor had returned*
almost unrecognizable from his journeys . . .

But before you get to that part you have to learn the names
you have to suffer not knowing anything about anyone

and slowly come to understand who each of them is, or who each of them
imagines him or her self to be —

and then, because you are the reader, you must try to understand who
you think each of them is because of who you believe yourself to be

in relation to their situation

or to your memory of one very much like it.

Oh it happens in time and time is hard to live through.
I can't read anything anymore, my dying brother said one afternoon,
not even letters. Come on, Come on, he said, waving his hand in the air,
What am I interested in — plot?

You come upon the person the author put there

as if you'd been pushed into a room and told to watch the dancing—

pushed into pantries, into basements, across moors, into
the great drawing rooms of great cities, into the small cold cabin, or

to here, beside the small running river where a boy is weeping,
and no one comes,

and you have to watch without saying anything he can hear.

One by one the readers come and watch him weeping by the running river,
and he never knows,

unless he too has read the story where a boy feels himself all alone.

This is the life you have written, the novel tells us. *What happens next?*

What We Would Give Up

One morning in Orlando Florida, I asked a group of college students—What would we be willing to give up to equalize the wealth in the world? Malls, a red-haired young woman said right away. Supermarkets, the young man in a black T-shirt said—where you go to buy bread, and there's a hundred and fifty loaves on the shelf. Imported fruit, the young woman sitting next to him said—berries in winter. A car, the guy with the nose ring said, I don't have a car anyway.

Travel? Jet fuel? Well, we'd all be together, someone said. TV, said the guy without a car, I don't watch TV anyway. What about coffee, I said, looking down at my double tall half-caf soy latte. Ok, everyone said, but I wondered about that one. Ten pairs of shoes? Yes. Movies? Maybe.

That week my phone was out of order. When the company tried to connect my line to a split line that would allow me fast cable access to the Internet everything went dead. When I called the phone company I was put on hold and had to listen to a tinny version of Vivaldi's *Four Seasons* pitched at what seemed a much faster than usual speed. *This call may be monitored.*

I was told to punch my number in five times during that first phone call, and every time I was transferred to a person who asked for my number again.

Eight calls that first day. We'll send a technician out, the central office would say. The technician, when he arrived would say, The problem is in the central office. When I called the central office, someone would say, We have to send a technician out. When I said, a technician has already been there, the central office person would say, All I can do is put in an order Ma'am. Vivaldi.

After seven days, I began to suspect that at the center of the central office is a room empty of all furniture but a table. On the table, a ringing telephone. Somewhere way down a long corridor, one guy in a broken chair in front of an empty desk. Every once in a while he cranes his neck towards the door and yells to no one in particular—is anyone gonna answer that?

If you don't want music, the phone company says, please hold through the silence.

When I came home from Orlando, the phone started working again. The Gap? Someone said. Everybody said, I don't go to The Gap.

Would I give up the telephone? Would I give up hot water? Would I give up makeup? Would I give up dyeing my hair? That was a hard one. If I stopped dyeing my hair everyone would know that my golden hair is actually gray, and my long American youth would be over—and then what?

Government

Standing next to my old friend I sense that his soldiers have retreated.
And mine? They're resting their guns on their shoulders
talking quietly.   I'm hungry, one says.
Cheeseburger, says another,
and they all decide to go and find some dinner.

But the next day, negotiating the too narrow aisles of
The Health and Harmony Food Store—when I say, Excuse me,
to the woman and her cart of organic chicken and green grapes
she pulls the cart not quite far back enough for me to pass,
and a small mob in me begins picking up the fruit to throw.

So many kingdoms,
and in each kingdom, so many people: the disinherited son, the corrupt
    counselor,
the courtesan, the fool.
And so many gods—arguing among themselves,
over toast, through the lunch salad
and on into the long hours of the mild spring afternoon—I'm the god.
No, I'm the god. No, I'm the god.

I can hardly hear myself over their muttering.

How can I discipline my army? They're exhausted and want more money.

How can I disarm when my enemy seems so intent?

Ordinary Time

A Thursday—no—a Friday someone said.
What year was it?
Just after the previous age ended, it began.
And although the scientists still studied the heavens
and the stars blazed—if the evening wasn't cloudy—
what happened did not occur in public view.
Some said it simply didn't happen, although others insisted they knew
    all about it
and made many intricate plans.

Poems from the Life of Mary

★

Sometimes the Moon Sat in the
Well at Night

Sometimes the moon sat in the well at night.
And when I stirred it with a stick it broke.
If I kept stirring it swirled like white
water, as if water were light, and the stick
a wand that made the light follow, then slow
into water again, un-wobbling, until
the wind moved it.
                    And I thought of all the moons
floating in the wells and rivers, spilling
over rocks where the water broke: moons
in the sheep water, the chicken water,
Or here or there an oar bent it, or a woman
spread out her skirt and let it pool there—
the light I mean, not the moon in a circle, not
the moon itself, but the light that fell from it.

Once or Twice or Three Times,
I Saw Something

Once or twice or three times, I saw something
rise from the dust in the yard, like the soul
of the dust, or from the field, the soul-body
of the field—rise and hover like a veil in the sun
billowing—as if I could see the wind itself.
I thought I did it—squinting—but I didn't.
As if the edges of things blurred—so what was in
bled out, breathed up and mingled: bush and cow
and dust and well: breathed a field I walked through
waist high, as through high grass or water, my fingers
swirling through it—or it through me. I saw it.
It was thing and spirit both: the real
world: evident, invisible.

How You Can't Move Moonlight

How you can't move moonlight—you have to go
there and stand in it. How you can't coax it
from your bed to come and shine there. You can't
carry it in a bucket or cup it in
your hands to drink. Wind won't

blow it. A bird flying through it won't
tear it. How you can't sell it or buy it
or save it or earn it or own it, erase
it or block it from shining on the mule's
bristly back, dog's snout, duck bill, cricket, toad.
Shallow underwater stones gleam underwater.

And the man who's just broken the neck
of his child? He's standing by the window
moonlight shining on his face and throat.

You Think This Happened Only Once
and Long Ago

You think this happened only once and long ago?
Think of a summer night and someone
talking across the water,

                      maybe someone
you loved in a boat, rowing. And you could
hear the oars dripping in the water, from
half a lake away, and they were far and
close at once. You didn't need to touch them
or call to them or talk about it later.
—the sky? It was what you breathed. The lake?
sky that fell as rain. I have been like you
filled with worry, worry—then relief.
You know the wind is sky moving. It happens all the time.

Annunciation

Even if I don't see it again—nor ever feel it
I know it is—and that if once it hailed me
it ever does—

And so it is myself I want to turn in that direction
not as towards a place, but it was a tilting
within myself,

as one turns a mirror to flash the light to where
it isn't—I was blinded like that—and swam
in what shone at me

only able to endure it by being no one and so
specifically myself I thought I'd die
from being loved like that.

My Mother's Body

Bless my mother's body, the first song of her beating
heart and her breathing, her voice, which I could dimly hear,

grew louder. From inside her body I heard almost every word she said.
Within that girl I drove to the store and back, her feet pressing

the pedals of the blue car, her voice, first gate to the cold sunny mornings,
rain, moonlight, snow fall, dogs . . .

Her kidneys failed, the womb where I once lived is gone.
Her young astonished body pushed me down that long corridor,

and my body hurt her, I know that—24 years old. I'm old enough
to be that girl's mother, to smooth her hair, to look into her exultant frightened
    eyes,

her bedsheets stained with chocolate, her heart in constant failure.
It's a girl, someone must have said. She must have kissed me

with her mouth, first grief, first air,
and soon I was drinking her, first food, I was eating my mother,

slumped in her wheelchair, one of my brothers pushing it,
across the snowy lawn, her eyes fixed, her face averted.

Bless this body she made, my long legs, her long arms and fingers,
our voice in my throat speaking to you now.

In the Course of the Last Three Days

She turned her face to the right
    opening her mouth as wide as it would go—so open
cupped open—so as to take in the most air—she was all body
    by then—a body that couldn't disguise its desire.

Under her toenails we discovered a forest—mushrooms stacked
    like white china plates.
And when she was dead
    we pulled the roses off the stems and scattered them over the sheet.

One of us touched her foot
One of us touched her shoulder
One of us tried to pull off her rings.
One of us tried to close her mouth by placing one hand on her head
and another hand under her chin, but her mouth wouldn't close.

Questions

Did you know your mother?

This morning, even before the light came, the birds started singing.

Who were you then?

I wrapped myself in the white sheet and stood on the top of the wooden stairs
  outside: the dawn slowly coming from the direction of the bay.

Did she touch you? Was she an affectionate person?

I called her name into the fold between night and day. I called it without
  expecting her to answer.

Limbo

We saw something once. And then it was over.
Time started up again as if it had never stopped.

We saw someone, and it was a soul.
and that soul was us, or I, or everyone.

We felt we had been waiting only after it had occurred.
And once it had happened we were homesick for before

and after—both. Then we stirred. We found we could move
what would have been our limbs.

Volition was the word we might have thought
if we'd been able to talk. (Talking makes thought possible,

someone told us later.) Without it one wanders
onto a bridge to nowhere which, now that I think of it,

might have been where we were—where I was

before whoever it was entered—then there was a door.
and beyond it—where we were apparently going.

Who

His steps up the stairs are like summer thunder one or two lakes away.
He comes like a scent rising from a night pond.
He comes like a recurring dream.
like the rain falling through the forest at night, and far away and through the
    trees
faint—the sound of fiddles
a square of light where a door opens to the dark.

The sound of his climbing is like breathing underwater
And the stumbling is an answer to a prayer no one heard.
Inevitable as daylight, exhaustive as pain,
his climb and his footfall sound like another world
ending
another world ending.

Non-violence

Some nights, long after we'd gone to sleep, our drunk father would wake us all up and order us to clean the kitchen. We'd stumble down to the counters and the dishwasher, blinking in our pajamas, dimwitted from sleep and embarrassed to look at each other. Let's do this quickly, someone would say, and then it will be over. And we'd get started—one wiping the counters, one sweeping, one washing pans, one drying, one stuffing the overflowing garbage into bags.

Sometimes that was it. We'd be back in our beds within the hour. Some nights, when we were done cleaning the kitchen, he'd say, Now clean the basement. We'd look at each other—was resistance worth the trouble tonight?—and without another word, head down the basement stairs.

One of those basement nights—was it one or two o'clock?—in a spirit of rising determination, we decided to sing. What did we sing? Some old Christmas carols? Did the boys sing too? It seems that all 8 of us did— picking up the broken toys, pulling the little school desks into rows again. Our father stood at the top of the basement stairs holding out his arms like Moses, saying to our mother—Listen to them singing. See? They're happy. They *want* to do it.

Sometimes, after we'd cleaned the kitchen and the basement, he'd say, Now clean the garage. And one of us would finally say, It's a school night Dad—and our spiritual victory, so carefully wrought and contained, would shatter—his fist would come down—we'd argue and scatter, and he'd rage around until he tired of it.

The nights went on and on. One night when he woke us all up, I asked the kids to sit down in a circle at the foot of the front stairs. We're just going to say No—if we're like Martin Luther King—if we all say no together, we'll win. Don't argue. Don't talk. Just hold hands.

Was I seventeen? Sixteen? My brother was a year older—tougher I thought, able to endure much. And when our father slapped the belt against the wall he didn't flinch. But when our father pulled one of the little girls to her feet—It's ok, she said, it's ok—I can take it—he was already walking towards the kitchen, kicking the back hall door open and the circle broke—the rest of us, one after the other, slowly getting up.

Justice before love, I'd say years later. What I meant was justice was love. That's what I thought then. What did I know? I would have sat there a long time, no matter what our father had done.

Non-violence 2

My daughter doesn't like the fly that keeps bugging her
as she eats her Cheerios this morning

but we had a talk about the ants yesterday, so she says,
The fly is alive, and I am alive, and covers her bowl

with a dish towel which she lifts a little every minute or so
so she can slip in her spoon.

But six hours later I want to murder that fly—landing on my arm
on my knee—want to find a book and flatten it.

This morning's newspaper says the British policeman checking
through the rubble of the bombed subway car thought,

because she was moaning, that the woman was alive. I don't want
to think about Donny who hung flies from his open desktop

and plucked off their wings,
or his gentle younger brother Bobby who killed himself when

he lost a lot of other people's money in the market.
My mother made a point, as she told the story, of mentioning he was

so considerate he pulled a plastic bag over his head before he did it.
A full summer day outside—hot, humid,

the fly that was bothering me, gone who knows where.
Now some detritus falling through the tree branches and air:

blossoms and seeds.

The Massacre

Someone hides in the bushes. Someone watches from the roof.
The men play with the sobbing women, tearing their dresses.
       Where is the kingdom of heaven?
Within that woman pushed from man to man?
Within each of the four men?
Last night, watching my daughter sleep, I felt my own
greater power and will rise, for no reason, within me:
Killing might stop time, I thought—to be death and not
for that moment, to fear it.
It moved through me like a clot—clear, cold,
and for an instant I knew myself—shouting in the careening
trucks with the rest of them
and what, in my exhilaration, I could become.

Before the Fire

Last night I lay on the floor of my friend's living room
and watched the burning cinders sift from the grate to the floor of the fireplace.

How good it was to look into the indifferent element.
What is fire, my friend said. Is it the log? is it something distinct from the log?

is it the log consuming itself? We lay there, adding one log after another until
the fire was ash.

My soul drank enough to know how thirsty it was.
This morning, the sunlight falling to the far corner of the bed, I remember

the dream of the forked stick—the divining stick that can find water. . . .
Susan, my old friend, put it into my hands, and I started across the yard

thinking to pretend to find what she wanted. But at a certain point
the thing pulled so hard I had to hold on, it pulled so hard towards the ground.

Fifty

The soul has a story that has a shape that almost no one
sees. No, no one ever does. All those kisses,

The bedroom chair that rocked with me in it, his body
his body and his and his and his.
                                        More, I said, more
and more and more. . . . What has it come to?
Like dresses I tried on and dropped to the floor. . . .

What the Woman Said

I don't want to offend anybody but I never did like
fucking all that much. Like I always say

the saw enjoys the wood more than the wood enjoys
the saw—know what I mean?
                                        I used to think

I could be like the girl in the movies—
then I watched myself—when it was happening—

my eyes closed, my head tilted back as if I were
him seeing me—and I couldn't feel anything.

I was watching me, and I was someone else who
looked like she was having a good time. Seems like

I spent years like that, watching him (whoever he was)
watching me—I have to admit

it was easier when he left. I'd watch myself watch him
leave and hear the strain of music swell up like a story.

watch myself walk back into the house and close the door
and lean against it.

I want to tell you everything I know about being alive but I
missed a lot of living that way—

My life was a story, dry as pages. Seems like he should have known
enough to lick them even lightly with his thumb

But he didn't. And I have to admit I didn't much like the idea
of telling him how.

New York City, October 2002

I spent a full hour last night longing for a man who
loved me 25 years ago, remembering his soft mouth and skin,
Mild-mannered school teacher—when I'd cry out
he'd cover my mouth with his hand.

The tar that bubbled in the far corner of the garage roof,
the lilies of the valley below the branches of the bushes in the backyard . . .
as soon as I write *taxi wheels on a wet road*—gone, before this line ends.

They waved white flags from the high windows—shirts? tablecloths?

And no matter how many things we buy—the small bag for the event,
bananas, books . . . hair in the sink, on the carpet, in the hairbrush,
hair in the tub.

The Man Who Kept Nightingales

His friend said something like, Let him go, he's done nothing.
—that's what the newspapers said.
And the nightingales sang as the car doors slammed slam slam, slam.

Do you want us to blow your brains out too? is what he said they said.
What did the man, who kept nightingales, say?
What did the dirt road say?
What comment from the bushes and plants and insects nearby?
And the rope? And the power tool?

The man's body, dumped by the sewage treatment plant, is speechless.
And the nightingales. What is the sound of that song?
I'm an American, I have never heard a nightingale sing,
although all the poems say the song of that bird is sublime.

Hurry

We stop at the dry cleaners and the grocery store
and the gas station and the green market and
Hurry up honey, I say, hurry hurry,
as she runs along two or three steps behind me
her blue jacket unzipped and her socks rolled down.

Where do I want her to hurry to? To her grave?
To mine? Where one day she might stand all grown?

Today, when all the errands are finally done, I say to her,
Honey I'm sorry I keep saying Hurry—
you walk ahead of me. You be the mother.

And, Hurry up, she says, over her shoulder, looking
back at me, laughing. Hurry up now darling, she says,
hurry, hurry, taking the house keys from my hands.

The Spell

(In memory of Elise Asher)

Our four-year-old neighbor Pablo has lost his wand
and so he tries to cast spells with his finger
which doesn't seem to work as well.

Then he brings handfuls of dimes and nickels to the couch
where I'm sitting, and when I say, Give me some money,
he says, No, laughing.

Give me some money, I say,
and he says, No.

Then he draws, on a piece of paper, a circle with a 10 inside
the word No, an unhappy mouth and eyes,
and gives that to me.

Why not ask the wand to find itself?
No, he says, shaking his head slowly.
Why not make a spell that will find it?
No, he says, that won't work.
What about this stick? his mother says, holding up a chopstick.
No, says Pablo, who knows the difference between what is secular and
what is sacred.

Every day when I pick up my four-year-old daughter from preschool
she climbs into her back booster seat and says, Mom—tell me your story.
And almost every day I tell her: I dropped you off, I taught my class
I ate a tuna fish sandwich, wrote e-mails, returned phone calls, talked with
    students
and then I came to pick you up.
And almost every day I think, My God, is that what I did?

Yesterday, she climbed into the backseat and said, Mom
tell me your story, and I did what I always did:
    I said I dropped you off
taught my class, had lunch, returned e-mails, talked with students. . . .
    And she said, No Mom, tell me the whole thing.

And I said, ok. I feel a little sad.
And she said, Tell me the whole thing Mom.
And I said, ok Elise died.

Elise is dead and the world feels weary and brokenhearted.
And she said, Tell me the whole thing Mom.
And I said, in the dream last night I felt my life building up around me and
    when I stepped forward and away from it and turned around I saw a high
    and frozen crested wave.

And she said, the whole thing Mom.

Then I thought of the other dream, I said, when a goose landed heavily on my
head—

But when I'd untangled it from my hair I saw it wasn't a goose but a winged
serpent

writhing up into the sky like a disappearing bee.

And she said, Tell me the whole story.

And I said, Elise is dead, and all the frozen tears are mine of course

and if that wave broke it might wash my life clear,

and I might begin again from now and from here.

And I looked into the rearview mirror—

She was looking sideways, out the window, to the right

—where they say the unlived life is.

Ok? I said.

And she said, Ok, still looking in that direction.

The Snow Storm

I walked down towards the river, and the deer had left tracks
deep as half my arm, that ended in a perfect hoof
and the shump shump sound my boots made walking made the silence loud.

And when I turned back towards the great house
I walked beside the deer tracks again.
And when I came near the feeder: little tracks of the birds on the surface
      of the snow I'd broken through.

Put your finger here, and see my hands, then bring your hand and put it in my side.

I put my hand down into the deer track
      and touched the bottom of an invisible hoof.
Then my finger in the little mark of the jay.

Mary (Reprise)

What is that book we always see—in the paintings—in her lap?
Her finger keeping the place of who she was when she looked up?

When I look up: my mother is dead, and my own daughter is calling
from the bathtub, Mom come in and watch me—come in here right now!

No Going Back might be the name of that angel—no more reverie.
Let it be done to me, Mary finally said, and that

was the last time, for a long time, that she spoke about the past.